ISBN 9780978821852
Published by Ncourageu2day
Book website: ncourageu2day.com/Author-Page
Contact: customerservice@ncourageu2day.com

I0182508

Dedication

I dedicate this book to you, my reader, because this book is deeper than poetry. You will read something that will encourage your heart and make your soul smile—

Contents

Chapter I

Arrows

The Tongue

God said...

And God saw— And

it was good!

What have you said? What have

you seen?

And was it good?

Slain In the Spirit

I fly with the eagles, run

with the gazelles, stand

under the rain.

By surprise,

His touch causes my eyes to blink

and blink,

then close.

Angels guide me to the floor—

Operated on by the Lamb.

I Die Daily

The more I hurt
the more I die.
The less I cry
The less I explain.
I don't know--
I just trust!

Smile Child!

If an egg falls and cracks,

It doesn't mean that it's the

END,

Especially if it's time

for new life to BEGIN.

No Vision

A boat on the sea without navigation is destined

to fail.

It'll allow the wind to take it anywhere

unless

The mercy of God prevails.

Decisions

We must be patient and not move hastily. We
must pray and get God's agenda for the day.

We must not make a quick decision and then look to God to
make a way.

Many times, this makes our lives hard, but in the struggle we
eventually learn.

When we do, His love, mercy and grace parts the Red Sea
and we pass through.

No Measure

You utter words and

things exist.

Hung the sun in the sky

'til the battle was won.

Put vision in my eyes so I can

see.

Your wisdom is infinite; I have

no measure for this

moment.

Sunday *(God)*

A canary can find a quiet spot

high in an Oak Tree

where there's safety and serenity—

I can find that same spot in you.

Monday

If you're frustrated because you're

stuck in traffic,

Look up and join the Blackbirds

sitting

peacefully on the power line as if they

own the highway.

Tuesday

If every day when you

go to work, Iago and

Roderigo

plot right at your side, you

better pray lest they

become successful.

Wednesday

Peace equals a

problem you apply a

solution

to that brings you

comfort.

Thursday

Success is connecting

your God-given abilities to the right generator

and just doing it.

Friday

Victory is when you can inhale the

synergy to

meet the challenges for today and

exhale your overwhelming yesterday.

Saturday

She laughs as

Sarah then

cries.

He's God and can

do a sudden thing!

Chapter 2

Me & Him

Perfect Love

Perfect love takes away all fears. This love is unconditional and everlasting. It's a love that would give its life for yours—a love that can be transformed into the Word you can trust the way an infant simply believes its parents for sustenance and protection.

It's this love you experienced when you found yourself on one side of the Red Sea and your desire on the other. You didn't fret but waited for the parting of the waters so you could meet some place in the middle.

And as you stood there, God separated you from your past, redeemed your present and showed you your future.

So here you are ready to accept this cup knowing that Pharaoh is still angry; that Nebuchadnezzar's furnace is still hot; that Haman still wants to destroy your family; and that there are still giants in your Canaan land.

So, what are you going to do? You're going to let perfect love cast out all fears for God has given you power over all the works of the enemy and has proclaimed that which he has joined together, let no man put asunder.

The Promise

When winter has gracefully covered you like a sheet of ice over a once thriving river, what will it take to break forth and flow again? Some would say Spring but...
It's the promise.

God told Abraham that He would make him the Father of many nations. But at 99 and Sarah not far behind, what was left for them to do since his wife was still barren?

They had to remember the promise when it seemed like all was lost for it lifted their spirits, renewed their youth and gave them strength.
Finally, Isaac came.

You both made a promise to each other, which was to love and cherish until death pulled you apart. Until then, this promise will cause your hands to grip, your bodies to embrace and your lips to touch.

Then your river will break forth and flow again.

Commanded to Love
Ephesians 5:22-33

Woman, submit.

I will love.

Out of me came you

with a womb.

Receive my seed and

You'll birth whatever I need.

What a mystery.

You don't have to love—

Just reverence me.

My Valentine

Jesus, will you be my valentine?
We'd go out on February 14, supernatural and wondrous
things we'll do. Seven P. M. will remain for 48 hours. It'll be a
night scientists will never understand.

We'll slip through Maryland, land in Barbados for dinner. At
evening's darkest hour, we'll go swimming in the Caribbean.
You'll light up the waters like the sun.

We'll explore the octopus and its spaghetti legs-- the eel and its
deadly shock. We won't worry about coming up for air.

New Testament wine we'll sip on—listen to some smooth jazz.
When the music stops, to Heaven we'll escape.

You'll show me the streets made of gold and where you sit on
the throne.

I'll see the four and twenty elders giving praise,
the Book of Life that holds my name.

You'll show me the Crystal Sea where the water is still as silence
and how the wind fears to disturb it.
Tomorrow, we'll slip to Africa!

Single Woman

Look only upon me— I'll be a
husband to thee.

Stop thinking about Ruth and Boaz, Adam and Eve or David
and Abigail—We must first get past Jesus and the Samaritan
Woman at the well.

I know you've been hurt and that you're tired, but I've held my
arms open for so long waiting for you to come in.
I only want to heal your wounds and give you shalom.

I'm thoughtful, sensitive, affectionate and dependable,
and I have no problems with commitment.

You'd never have to fear the terror of night or the arrow that
flies by day when you become a bride of the Almighty for, I
am Elohim, El-Shaddai, El-Elyon and Adonai—

I made you and I can supply—
I possess the heavens and the earth, and I am the same yesterday,
today and forever.

Single Man

I haven't forgotten about you.
Remember, I gave Eve to Adam even though
he may have been content keeping the garden.

I haven't forgotten about you.
Remember, I brought Rebekah to Isaac even though
he may have been content being forty
and heir of my everlasting covenant.

I haven't forgotten about you.
Remember, I gave Abigail to David even though
she may have been content being
separated from a fool.

I haven't forgotten about you. Remember,
I drew you to me, so be content.
I'm not a respecter of persons,
and I'm always on time.

How to Be Free
(analogy)

Take the Bible and turn to Genesis 1:26—
It tells you who you are. Now take the contents of Your brain
and pour it in a sifter.

Shake out all the lies and thoughts of low
self-esteem. Pour the remains in a bowl
and mix it with four cups of love for self.

Add in two cups of purpose to begin your
journey. Add two tablespoons of vanilla *favor*—
No lemon or anything sour.

Add six eggs, but first remove the
yokes.

Gradually add the milk to help renew
the mind.

Time for baking to destroy
the shackles.

When finished, return contents to the head
so the body can experience liberty.

Me & Him

In solitary,
sing like a canary.
Do my holy dance—
Pen ready to write.

On His bosom,
rests my head.
Listen to His voice—
The world in His hand.

Kiss His holy face,
Mine in return.
Difficult to stand—
Relax in the Jacuzzi.

Archive the moments,
Beauty well spoken.
Mercy, no man can give—
Protection from an army ant.

Wisdom that confounds,
Too much joy for the body.
Intimacy--
Do not disturb.

In The Beginning

Separated from our Heavenly Father then from each other into a world of sin but not without instructions no matter how forgotten.

Through confusion, failure, rejection, loneliness, some joy and laughter, we were drawn back to our Master where His spirit returned destiny to our remembrance.

Individually we began the journey and then one day we met. I didn't recognize you, and I'm unsure if you knew me. Silently your rib kept pulling at my heart. Then the anesthesia kicked in.

You fell asleep and when you awoke, I was at your side to help fulfill your vision, which will leave a divine legacy behind.

His Glory

It's not the sassy way
she wears her hair or
the color of her eyes
and how they blink.

It's not her voice although
it may sound sweet.
Nor how she smells
although it's Eternity.

It's not her sexy body
or the way she walks.
It's the glory of God
On the inside.

Jesus

I Love you so much.
I love your charm.
I love your touch.

Your tender mercies are so many,
compassionate and forgiving you are.
Your joy is overwhelming.

Your peace surpasses all understanding.
You walk closely with me in the valley
to dispel all shadows of death.
When we are together,
I feel so safe—

You would protect me from an insect.
When we leave this ecstasy,
I know I will be faced with people,
pressures and problems, but
Even then, I will not worry—
You handled them all on the cross.

Invitation

There I sat. I had a window seat. It was a romantic
moonlight dinner. The music was playing softly.

The stars shinned brightly in the clear, dark sky. I sat patiently.
Then He spoke softly into my
ear, "I love you and want to show you how much
I care.

I waited for this moment year after year. Until now, I protected
you and kept you near my heart. I watched you every day as I
allowed circumstances to usher you along the way.

One day, you invited me in to stay. A new love had
begun. Yes, you were unsure about exactly what to do,
but I kept wooing you all the way through.

So here we are at last—the old you is now a thing of the
past. I tarried for this moonlight dinner for so long--a quite
night without any interruptions from the phone--just you and
me gazing through the window.

From this point on, I will hear you when you cry and will wipe
all tears from your eyes. I want nothing more than a
relationship--happiness

between you and me. Yes, there will be work to do, but
remember that I will never leave or forsake you. My covenant
with you is written in blood, and there could be no greater
love.

Trust me in all your situations knowing that my Words will give
you the breakthrough. They have been exalted above my

name--none will return unto me in vain.

There isn't a star in the sky that I am not aware of if it should fall, so remember; if you need me, just call. At last, I have my love once and for all."

Goodness & Mercy

I was once in sin but through the redemptive blood of Jesus,
God took me back in. My mind is constantly being transformed
by the Word. The things I used to do; I can't do anymore. The
blood of Jesus caused me to shut every door.

My body is not my own--for it was purchased with a price and
now I present it a living and holy sacrifice. I am now an heir
and co-laborer of Jesus Christ. I have good health, prosperity,
peace, and I live the abundant life.

I give distractions no place for I know in whom I set my face.
Test trials and tribulations—Let them have their way. They only
make me closer to Jesus anyway. My soul rejoices in the Lord
for He is the All-Knowing One.

He told Abraham He would make him a Father of many
nations; therefore, I know He will also reveal my destination. I
put my trust in Him and have no fear—For He is my
habitation, and I do not let the devil come in with any trick of
condemnation.

I sing praises to His name-- I give
Him all the glory--
He prevented my life from being a horror
story.

In His Image

You were made in the image
after the likeness of God.
There is no one else like you.

God knew who you were in the secret Place—
Your frame was already known to Him.

No problem or situation can get you down—
You have the power to change the things that be.

You can bind, and you can loose.
You are not moved by any mountain
you can cast in the sea.

You know who you are in Christ,
so, love you and be free!

Pink Rose

Drowning in my tears, I cried out to my friend.
He came and filled my heart with such side-
cracking joy. Afterwards He said,

"You are a rose from the Garden of Eden—
a pink rose with bright petals that still have the morning
dew gleaming all over them.

Your smell is sweet and savory.
Everything around you enjoys your presence
because of your heavenly air."

Love, The Holy Spirit

Chapter 3

Portraits

Portraits are poems I've written about people I've encountered since 1994. This encounter ranged from five minutes to several years.

Most of the names that inspired these poems have been removed, so you can conveniently insert your name if you're in need of encouragement.

How precious to me are your thoughts, O God! How vast is the sum of them! Were I to count them, they would outnumber the grains of sand. When I awake, I am still with you. Ps 139:17-18 (NIV)

A Friend

Modern day Harriett Tubman, paving the way for others to follow from a healthy freedom walk to just plain straight talk.

Her journey has left her discerning, strong and wise, so she doesn't hesitate to encourage a weary traveler that staggers by her side.

She arrives to work with the radiance of sunshine; energy of Wonder Woman and a sassy style all of her own.

She tries to give everyone respect, but if they reject it, she will not be the one walking away with a yoke around her neck.

Every day for her is a new beginning filled with excitement and possibilities, which is what happens when you have the liberty, love and creative nature of God.

Joyful Son

Exempted from some of the cocoon metamorphosis, you came
out a thriving butterfly--A combination of what your parents
possessed.

You bring moisture to parched land; sweet melodies to bitter
silence and hope to a plum dying in the sun.

You're as Josiah who reigned at eight; as Jesus who drew the
little children and as David who slew the lion and the bear.

Abundant encouragement you sow into
the lives of others, but it doesn't always come back on every
wave, so when you're in
a season of drought, don't get discouraged— Just read these
words and keep sowing.

Humble Servant

Power in reserve is what comes to mind when I think of you, for
you possess a meekness that can only come from being crushed
under extreme weight like a piece of coal found in the
mountains of South Africa. But when it has withstood the
process, the diamond breaks forth on divine assignment.

I've watched how you've facilitated a room full of egos and
guided them into your vision as a shepherd leading sheep.
You knew where you were going and who'd take you there,
so when people got off course, you'd display the nature of a
diplomatic Lion and then returned to the humble Lamb.

When God uses you mightily, you quickly slip through the
crowd while everyone remains in a stupor under the cloud.
You'd rather that God got all the glory in lieu of the dust
settling with man pumping your flesh.

I know you're peculiar because of whom you serve, but it's
also evident that your well runs very deep, which is why I see you
as power in reserve.

Sound of the Trumpet

Mighty man of God who is also a man of war for when you
lift your voice unto the Most High, shackles are destroyed
and burdens are removed--Jericho walls fall down and
many wounded hearts cease to bleed.

Over two thousand years ago before you entered into your
mother's womb, God chose you to express Himself in song so
captives could be set free.

You didn't have to audition or show Him your resume. He
simply looked through the blood of Jesus and saw His image
and likeness and equipped you with all that you would
need.

A man of worship and praise usually finds himself under some
sort of attack but always remember that you're trained for this
and the battle is already won.

You have a friend who sticks closer than any brother. You
have a Heavenly Father who will never leave or forsake you.

You have a God who supplies all your needs, and He's given you goodness and mercy to follow you all the days of your life.

I encourage you to continue to allow the apothecary to make your anointing sweeter and sweeter, because there is a harvest of people waiting on this Son of God to sound his trumpet so they can be set free.

Processed

When I look at you, I see two pieces of coal that were processed by tremendous pressure from the Colorado Mountains and then blended into one gracious diamond.

Like two cubes of ice melted into one cup of water, you can be poured upon a thirsty plant or a deprived soul.

You remind me of Adam and Eve before and after the fall because through it all, you remained together.

As the sun's rays motivate plants to rise from beneath the earth, your very presence speaks volumes of comfort and encourages others that God is real and that they can reach higher.

May you both continue to let your candles burn as one for your light will leave a legacy behind that cannot be counted.

Pastors and Teachers

You and all the teachers have walked worthy of the vocation
in which you were called, because we've been powerfully
influenced by the fruits of your labor.

As a result, we just want to say thank you for six
sanctifying qualities that you've displayed.

First, it takes obedience just to say yes and answer the
call. We know that "yes" meant suffering for His cause but
nevertheless it's an honor, because many are called but
few are chosen.

Secondly, it takes love—an unconditional love
that's committed to seeing that others know who God is and
what it takes to have a relationship with Christ and experience
the power that comes when we walk in His image.

Thirdly, it takes faith to believe that your labor is not in vain and
that what you teach falls on good ground in which the Lord
has and will cause a harvest to spring forth in our hearts.

Fourthly, it takes patience. For as you give the Word to us to
effect change, we know God is doing the same in you.

So, when the enemy tries to make you feel unworthy, remind him that you were chosen before the fall of Adam and that you know clearly where your humanity ends and God's divinity begins.

Fifthly, I applaud you for your discipline to study the Word, to pray, to worship and do all that is required to cultivate your relationship with the Lord so His teaching anointing can be activated and poured upon us.

Lastly, it takes humility—a death to you so that others can live and grow. You've evidently received the rhema that the greatest among us is to be the least. So go forth in this next season with these words in your heart:

"And they shall teach my people the difference between the holy and the profane, and cause them to discern between the unclean and the clean." Ezekiel 44:23.

Agape Love

Who can find a virtuous Shepherd of God? For not only does the heart of her husband safely trusts in her and her children rise up and call her blessed, but she has sheep and other sheep that honors her as well.

She provides her people with wisdom and understanding that distill as the dew, as showers upon thirsty grass and as tiny rain upon the fragile herb.

She has the warrior spirit of Deborah, the beauty and courage of Queen Esther, a worshipping heart as King David, the Spirit of the Lion and the Lamb and the agape love of God.

This love motivates her to go deep into the valley of dry bones where she releases faith in the Word of God knowing the gathered shall become assembled and delivered. Never is there hesitation to breathe her life into barren and hopeless areas to bring about wholeness.

Then as any good shepherd, she watches them, with staff and rod, become an active member in the Body of Christ.

Chosen by God

Give me a man with a heart to emancipate his people and I'll make him a leader and load him down with silver and gold as I did with Moses.

Give me a lady with a heart to risk her life for her people and I'll entrust her with favor, influence and honor as I did with Queen Esther.

Give me a man who could have asked for anything in the world but instead he asked for wisdom to lead my people and I'll entrust him with authority and riches as I did with King Solomon.

Give me a man who has a heart to simply trust me no matter what conditions he finds himself in and I'll have people coming from near and far to trade with him as I did with Joseph.

Give me a lady in great debt that would give her last meal to my prophet instead of keeping it for herself and I'll make her an entrepreneur over night as I did with the Widow Woman.

Give me a very wise, compassionate and unselfish man with a heart to see people empowered, and I'll entrust him with wealth, power and people as I did with you.

Coworker

Crafted from a mixture of Bill Gates, Nicholas Cage and Steven Seagull arrives a talented and clever, Windows-troubleshooting, no nonsense, confident, Harley Davidson riding man.

Life's experiences have taken him on a world tour that has replaced anxiety, fear and intimidation with what true happiness is all
about--a greater appreciation for life and others; wisdom and understanding and how to relax and have fun.

He's a determined and proactive person who can create the doors he needs to walk through, which makes him an asset wherever he is.

Marriage

In a world where you trade your partner when you get bored; leave because you don't have the patience to deal with unresolved issues or because the calories look lower on the other body; how does one remain together?

The answer is derived from adding $2 + 1$, which gives you a three-fold cord that can't easily be broken—you, your spouse and God. Because you knew how to keep your positions at the base of your triangle while looking up and consulting the Father, your marriage became a witnessing tool to those who believed it couldn't be done.

It's an encouragement to couples thinking about uniting. It's a testimony to yourself and others that God is faithful and what He's joined together produces harmonious fruits of destiny.

I'm sure this journey had some turbulence, but the Apothecary allowed it to prepare your costly anointing that will set single and married captives free.

I salute you on years of marriage, and you'll have many more because you know how to add $2 + 1$.

Directors

Like diamonds, you all have been subjected to years of tremendous pressure and heat then extracted from various rough stones to be cut and polished into the brilliant gems to which I now speak.

You've taken experiences from your journey and administered wisdom to those in need. Your excellent performance becomes evident

When I see the respect you receive; When I see your

knowledge being valued; When I see trust placed in

your decisions; When I see confidence in your

integrity;

When I see appreciation shown for your ideas and when I see those around you continue to excel.

As precious diamonds, continue to let your brilliant rays permeate those you direct.

Well Done

From my womb, you came forth--a son who is ambitious, hardworking, dedicated, caring sensitive and giving. You make being a mother so rewarding.

Life doesn't stand still--it moves so fast. It seems like only yesterday that you were in my arms, and now you have produced a new generation from your loins.

As my son, you have made me very proud, and today, I honor you as a father-- The priest of your household--The one who will reveal God to your children-- The one who is your family's provider and protector.

As you continue on in your journey as a father, never fear or worry, because God will never leave or forsake you. Continue to have the attitude of Joshua who stood up as the Priest in his house and declared:

"As for me and my house, we will serve the Lord."

May you always be blessed in the city and blessed in the field and in your coming and going. Love always, Mom.

The Manager

A distinguished and dapper manager who relates to
people with a confident and warm assertiveness--

His ambidextrous assets are displayed when he uses keen
judgment while flowing in unforgettable compassion.

He's like a tree firmly supported by much integrity. From his
branches extend support and encouragement for his team;

He blossoms with precision and understanding in unique
situations; He has a wealth of knowledge he releases freely, and
his charisma can motivate a snail.

He and professionalism are synonymous; He's a
legacy and will have this impact everywhere.

Oil and Wine

Two beautiful branches abiding in the true
vine;

Together you bring forth much fruit-- the kind that
remains.

With just your touch, rivers of living water begin to pour out. With
just a whisper in the ear, one becomes Holy Ghost filled;

With your tender embrace, yokes are broken and shackles are
removed. From just a song ringing from your voice, joy is
restored and broken hearts are healed.

With your anointed word being preached, minds are renewed
to bring glory to the King.

You are God's ministers of flaming fire, and He
will never leave or forsake you and will continue
to empower you.

Stillbirth

The conception of your child brought you great joy, but when the child passed through your womb, there were periods of great pain.

But shortly after the birth, you looked for joy again. That was when the doctor placed the baby in your arms.

When we meet someone special, a form of conception takes place. However, there may be times when problems inevitably arise. Then we're thrown into labor.

You've been in labor for quite a while and now that you've experienced stillbirth, you must release the pain.

Even though you may not understand, I pray that you'll extend your arms so the Great Physician can restore your joy.

Faith

Periodically the atmosphere releases a distinguished,
inarticulate sound that's deeper than a response to something
comical and more effective than some medicines.

It's the sound of your laughter. It stems from a wellspring
bubbling with obstacle removing power that overflows to
conquer life's uncertainties.

Its foundation is layered with confidence and uninhibited
freedom that refuses to be entrapped by fear that would try
and stalk this risk taker.

It's the sound of a well-balanced leader who exudes to his
followers how one should dress whether it's Winter, Spring,
Fall or Summer.

She works diligently without looking for man's flattery--she knows someone higher will ensure her an exceeding reward.

She keeps her staff well informed, and her concentration is devoted completely to a task like a silk cocoon in creation.

She's like Moses who was careful and detailed to ensure that the tabernacle was made after the pattern.

Like Nehemiah, she has a passion to provide physical stability to a place of affliction. If given the resources, she can assemble a labor force to rebuild city walls.

As with any great endeavor, she will meet opposition. I encourage her to meet the challenge with boldness, wisdom and an invincible determination to complete the task!

The Captain

He's the captain of a new ship and he's about to
take a journey to a place called Success.

His crew members will be navigators that can handle deep
waters--they'll remain optimistic and determined when
facing a storm.

If lightening were to strike and damage the hull, they'd turn up the
synergy until all repairs were done.

Whether the skies are intensely raging or vividly calm, he'd make
sure everyone laughed and had fun.

His crew will enjoy the incentives he'd place in their hands;
although, their greatest incentive will lie within . . .

The consuming passion to see this ship reach its expected end!

Sister

I've seen you release the power to dream larger than the Pacific
Ocean.

You have the tenacity and faith to launch forth to make your
dreams tangible when others allowed past fears to rob or
delay them of their dreams and goals.

You always challenge your innovative mind to find ways to
leap over hurdles that stand in your way, and you create doors
that don't exist so you can walk through them.

You have boldness that I greatly admire— a boldness that
isn't hindered by the thoughts or on-looks of others.

It's a boldness that demonstrates one of your thought
processes…"I've envisioned it. I believe it. I will achieve it…"

You're like a surviving soldier that I've seen betrayed, angry,
hurt, confused, and sometimes lonely. But most importantly,
I've seen you leap over those walls and run through troops and
then forgetting those things which were behind you

and pressing towards a greater reason for being.

Your life has been an inspiration to me, and I desire nothing less than continued success, joy and happiness as you continue to create the legacy that only **you** were meant to leave on this earth. Keep dreaming, believing and achieving!

A Gift

You are always discerning and ready to speak life into the
spirits of the wounded and heavy laden.

You encourage them to go on because you know the
world--Jesus has already overcome.

You are a listening ear to the oppressed--open arms of love
for the broken hearted you embrace. When they leave your
presence, they are ready to go on.

Your warrior prayers are a bridge for many faced with troubled
waters. You run to the battle knowing God's Word will
perform all that it says.

Faithful and committed--that's who you are. You
will go the distance no matter how far.
You are a gift to the body of Christ-- A woman of God that is
strong and wise. Remain one with God and keep touching
many lives.

You have what it takes to keep them focused on the prize.

Psalmist

You are as beautiful as a flower operating in God's power.
You flow with such love, compassion, mercy & grace.

From out of you emerge anointed songs that have been tested
in the fire. They touch our hearts and open our eyes--they set
us free and cause us to experience freedom and walk in true
liberty.

I thank God for you and the ministry he has called you to. May
you always be blessed and continue to walk side by side with the
Holy Spirit.

Super Senior

In the beginning God made A great
light to reign in the day,
A great light to reign in the night and A great
person to reign in His sight.

I've always known you as a shinning reflection of His joy,
encouragement, love, His faithfulness, compassion and keeping
power.

You're a radiant rose bush that was plucked up and replanted
by the rivers of living waters where God has not allowed
boisterous winds

To break you or blow away your tender petals. He's kept you
in a place where all your needs were supplied and where your
wants couldn't be denied.

You're a highly favored Daughter of Zion and it's an honor to
know you and have this opportunity to celebrate another year
of your life!

Mom

Children are a blessing. They are a gift from God.
Hannah prayed earnestly that she might conceive. When
God remembered Rachel, her womb was opened too.

When Sarah and Elisabeth thought It was over
God let them know He wasn't through.
Mary wondered how she would conceive being she knew not
a man, but God revealed to her His master plan.

All of these women are mothers just like you. Your story may not
appear in the Bible, but you are special too! He was there with
you in the hospital room, and He opened up your womb.

Many times, after the children are born, moms can feel
forgotten--it seems as if only you remember the struggles
you went through.

Never be discouraged or dismayed for when you see Jesus, He
will say, "You trained my children up in the way they should
go, and you did not spare the rod when they were wrong--
Don't worry about another ultrasound...Just come up
hither and receive your crowns."

Kingdom Woman

When the wall of Jerusalem is broken down and the gates are burned with fire, that's when you need a Kingdom Woman like you to help restore and overcome the enemy.

When you've been called to the front lines as Barak with the assurance of victory, yet you lack confidence, that's when a Kingdom Woman can assist you on your journey.

When your people are about to be destroyed for a lack of knowledge at the hand of the enemy, that's when you need a Kingdom Woman who knows she's been born for such a time as this to address the king even if she perishes.

Out of the furnace of much affliction are these types of women chosen. They don't lick their battle wounds for years to come, but is motivated to help others be set free. Their rewards come when they see folk go from faith to faith and from glory to glory.

Their rewards come when they see the gospel preached to the poor; when they see the brokenhearted healed; when they see the captives set free; when they see sight given to the blind; when they see the oppressed set at liberty.

Their rewards come when they look back at their own lives and see how the Lord brought them through with resurrection power and without the smell of smoke on them.

You are a Kingdom Woman and are appreciated for how the Lord uses you to reach one and teach one.

Clutch Man (DH)

When your team is down by a few winning points with seconds on the clock, you're the kicker that gives the team the winning field goal.

When your team is down by a few winning points with seconds on the clock, you're the QB that throws into the end zone for a touchdown.

When your team is down by a few winning points with seconds on the clock, you're the receiver that catches the ball in the ball in the end zone.

When the team is down by a few winning points with seconds on the clock, you're the shooter who sends up the winning three pointer.

When the team is in the 10th frame in need of a strike, you're the anchor man who finishes with a turkey—three strikes.

When the team is in the last inning of the game and have three players on base, you're the player that hits the home run.

In a family, nothing is perfect but what counts is commitment and getting the win for the team, and I believe that we have a winning team.

For You

Who can find a virtuous woman? Nobody can unless God makes them first, and that's what he did in you. Holy, creative, resourceful, confident, courageous, loving, and kindness are in your DNA.

Your face radiates glory--His glory like the sun. As the blood pumps through your veins and sustains your life, it also resuscitates the living dead. You give to those in need. You wrap your loving arms around bleeding hearts. You encourage parched souls. You sing songs to the weary. You help others to bear their crosses.

You laugh when you want to cry. You encourage rather than becoming angry. You sacrifice rather than being selfish. You rise to every occasion rather than shrinking back.

You've done well, so enjoy God's rest as he strokes your face with his mentholated breeze. Enjoy his fresh dew every morning. Smell his pink roses in the afternoon and enjoy *his son* every night. Shalom my friend.

Chapter 4

Seasons

Question?

Is Jesus the reason for the season or is the season

the reason for Jesus or does Jesus need a

season to be celebrated?

Is it time for me to receive or is it time

for me to give?

If I give, who should be the recipient?

If I receive, am I the one being celebrated?

The Significance of You

(Woman)

When God said,

"Be fruitful and multiply" He

knew the Significance of you.

When He needed to come Down

as the Son of Man, He knew the

Significance of you.

He is God and could have chosen

another way but He wanted to

show the significance of you.

Your Creation

Oh, wow Daddy, I love what I see--monument mountains
and Grand Canyon valleys that create an enticing pathway to
a horizon so far-- makes you want to leap off this Patapsco
stone wall and walk on the air just to fall back into reality but
not hard because the bushes below appear really cushy.

Steroid injected trees that tried to reach Heaven could have
only been created by the Ancient of Days. Crowded with
dark green hands reaching out into nowhere just grabbing at
the atmosphere. Sun so far but yet impacting all that's near and
open--Indirectly all that's behind the shadows.

Sounds of insects and chirping birds in harmony with this
supernatural forest ambiance. A massaging breeze that could
quickly rock you to sleep like anesthesia, but this is where I
ended up in search of a place to read, enjoy nature, meditate
on who God created me to be and what's inside of me.

All my thoughts led me back to Him and how He meticulously
created these trees down to my beautifully crafted toes to walk
on His land and perpetually be in awe.

Enjoy the Moments

Enjoy the moments for soon they will be gone...

Embrace it with all your heart so it can be a cherished memory. It saddens the soul when you remember how you raced through the moments.

Earn the fulfillment of the hour by making your mind focus on where you are. You leave uncompensated when you race through the moments.

Edify yourself with what surrounds you. You miss out on so much when you race through the moments.

Educe the hidden beauty waiting to be exposed that so many people neglected when they raced through the moments.

Electrocute the pressures that say you don't have time to savor and avoid disappointments of an unseasoned event by not racing through the moments.

Explode with enthusiasm about what you are doing instead of racing through the moments.

Emancipate the creativity within that must be deposited here. Racing through the moments aborts its destination.

Employ what has been set before you or did you even notice
it...racing through the moments?

Endear that friend in your life and appreciate whatever
stage. Racing through the moments will cause that friend to
go astray.

Exhort a peer or a stranger who may be in your circle; however,
if you race through the
moments, you probably won't notice their countenance.

Examine who is reading this poem. Is it causing you to think, or
are you racing through the moments?

Exist in the now and enjoy the moments. You
don't know what's in the next minute or hour.
When you race through the moments, you forget who allowed
you to be where you are and if He'll allow you to enter
tomorrow.

Sympathy

There are never enough words or the right words to really comfort someone when they've lost a loved one.

Yes, family and friends can be there to express their condolences, but are there ever enough words to bring true consolation to their soul?

There is someone however that you and I both share who can give you exactly what you need. But in a time of bereavement, we really don't want to focus on that still small voice as our face floods with tears.

So, after you have mourned for a while, remember to grab hold of the Horns of the Altar and allow God to pour in the oil and the wine so your fragile heart can heal, because He identified with your loss when He was separated from His Son on the cross.

Bio

Patricia Houston is a writer who finds inspiration in God's creations and the beauty in others. With a passion for encouraging people, Patricia has been sharing her positive outlook since 1994. She is a member of the New Psalmist Baptist Church and a proud graduate of the University of Baltimore, Johns Hopkins University, and Regent University. In addition to her roles as a child of God, wife, mother, and minister, Patricia enjoys reading, writing, nature, bowling, traveling, skating and teaching.